Date: 2/14/12

Slimy • Scaly • Deadly
Reptiles and Amphibians

AMPHIBIANS

Gareth Stevens
Publishing

Please visit our Web site www.garethstevens.com. For a free color catalog of all our high-quality books, call toll free 1-800-542-2595 or fax 1-877-542-2596.

Library of Congress Cataloging-in-Publication Data
Amphibians / Tim Harris, editor.
     p. cm. — (Slimy, scaly, deadly reptiles and amphibians)
    Includes index.
    ISBN 978-1-4339-3441-4 (library binding) — ISBN 978-1-4339-3442-1 (pbk.)
    ISBN 978-1-4339-3443-8 (6-pack)
    1. Amphibians—Juvenile literature. I. Harris, Tim.
  QL644.2.A474 2010
  597.8—dc22   2009037192

Published in 2010 by
Gareth Stevens Publishing
111 East 14th Street, Suite 349
New York, NY 10003

© 2010 The Brown Reference Group Ltd.

For Gareth Stevens Publishing:
Art Direction: Haley Harasymiw
Editorial Direction: Kerri O'Donnell

For The Brown Reference Group Ltd:
Editorial Director: Lindsey Lowe
Managing Editor: Tim Harris
Children's Publisher: Anne O'Daly
Design Manager: David Poole
Designer: Sarah Williams
Production Director: Alastair Gourlay
Picture Researcher: Clare Newman

Picture Credits:
Front Cover: Shutterstock: Eric Isselee, Shutterstock: Maxim Petrichuk.

Creatas: 11b; Shutterstock: John Bell 13b, Darren Green 19t, Eric Isselee TP, Andre Klaassen 22b, Robyn Mackenzie 14cl, Phil Morley 6b, Dr Moreley Read 12c, 17b, 18t, Steve Simzer 10b, Snowleopard 4, Michael Steden 20c, Pawel Strykowski 20b.

All Illustrations © The Brown Reference Group plc

Publisher's note to educators and parents: Our editors have carefully reviewed the Web sites that appear on p. 31 to ensure that they are suitable for students. Many Web sites change frequently, however, and we cannot guarantee that a site's future contents will continue to meet our high standards of quality and educational value. Be advised that students should be closely supervised whenever they access the Internet.

Manufactured in the United States of America
1 2 3 4 5 6 7 8 9   12 11 10

CPSIA compliance information: Batch #BRW0102GS: For further information contact Gareth Stevens, New York, New York at 1-800-542-2595.

Contents

Where does a Surinam toad carry its eggs?

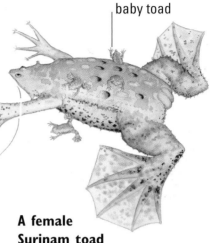

baby toad

A female Surinam toad

Surinam toads live in lakes in South America. After mating, the male toad rides on the female's back while she swims loops in the water. She produces an egg at the top of each loop. On the way back around, the male scoops the egg from the water and pushes it onto the female's spongy back. The back swells up to hold the eggs in pockets. The tadpoles stay in their pockets until they are fully developed into toads.

Female koikoi poison frogs carry tadpoles on their backs, too.

Do you know...?

Midwife toads live in warm parts of Europe. These toads also carry their eggs while they are developing. It is the males that do this job. They carry the eggs glued to their legs.

What are the Asian horned toad's horns for?

Asian horned toads live in the forests of Malaysia and Indonesia. The toad has two points sticking out of its head above each eye. These are the toad's "horns." The toad's snout ends in a similar point. The toad's body has a rough fringe around it and several similar ridges. All these features make the toad's body look like a bundle of brown leaves. The Asian horned toad's camouflage keeps it hidden among the dead leaves on the forest floor.

An Asian horned toad

Do you know...?

Scientists think that about half of all species of frogs and toads are under threat of extinction. In recent decades more than 150 species have died out. The main causes are habitat loss and a fungal disease.

Leaf litter, where Asian horned toads live

What is a spadefoot?

Spadefoot toads spend most of their time in fields, where they prey on bugs. They are most active at night. During the day, the toads hide away in burrows. At dawn, they dig a new den in the soft ground, using a spade-shaped bone on the heels of the back feet. This structure forms the "spadefoot" in the toad's name. The toad lowers itself backward into the ground. The soil falls into the burrow on top of the toad. The toad digs itself out again using a bony plate on its head.

A Syrian spadefoot leaping

Do you know...?

The spadefoot toads that live in dry habitats breed in the pools and puddles made by summer rain. The males call to females to come to the pools. These calls can be heard more than 1 mile (nearly 2 km) away.

A common spadefoot

What's the difference between a frog and a toad?

Amphibians are a group of animals that live in both water and on land. Amphibians without tails form a group of animals called anurans. This group is better known as frogs and toads. There is no simple way of telling a toad from a frog. Toads generally have rounded bodies and shorter legs than frogs. Many toads also have large lumps, or warts, on their backs and walk rather than hop.

A European common toad

Do you know...?

African clawed toads, or common platannas, spend their whole life in water. They have large lungs and can stay underwater for several minutes at a time. The toads have huge webbed hind feet, but their front feet have four long fingers for gripping food. The toads have poisonous skin that makes them taste bad to fish.

Why are cane toads so common in Australia?

A cane toad

The cane toad is one of the largest toads in the world. Cane toads originally came from South America, but were taken to Australia to eat the beetles that were damaging sugarcane crops there. The toads ate the beetles and a lot of other animals, too. The toads bred quickly, and today they are pests themselves.

Do you know...?

Harlequin toads are colorful animals that live in mountain forests in South America. There are about sixty species of harlequin toads, and they range in color from bright yellow to blue and red. The toads are named for clowns from the Middle Ages who performed in very colorful outfits.

Where is a frog's eardrum?

Frogs have ears, but it is not easy to see them. Most of a frog's ear is inside its head. Like the ears of other animals, a frog's ear works using a thin piece of skin called an eardrum. Sound makes the eardrum vibrate, and the rest of the ear converts these

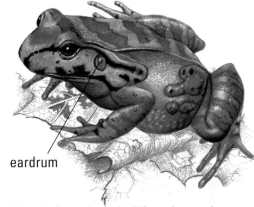

eardrum

A South American bullfrog has a large eardrum on each side of its head.

vibrations into a signal that is sent to the brain. A frog's eardrums are on the sides of its head. In most species, it is easy to see the eardrums.

Do you know...?

As their name suggests, bullfrogs are large frogs. They are hunters that prey on many small animals, such as beetles, mice, and even smaller frogs. They hunt mainly at night. As well as having good hearing, bullfrogs also rely on their sensitive eyes to find prey. Just like a cat's eyes, a bullfrog's eyes (right) have a shiny inner lining to catch as much light as possible. This lining makes their eyes glow red in certain kinds of light.

How do frogs croak?

Frogs are noisy creatures. During the mating season, male frogs attract females by producing loud croaks. Each kind of frog has its own call. The calls are made using a sac of stretchy skin in the throat. The frog fills this sac with air, making it puff up like a balloon. It then squeezes the air through a narrow part of the throat. This makes a loud noise, just like a balloon does when the air empties out.

Do you know...?

Bush squeakers are tiny frogs that live in South Africa. They are named for their squeaky calls, which sound more like a grasshopper than a frog.

A male frog fills his throat sac.

Do any frogs have a tail?

Adult frogs are amphibians without tails. But a baby frog, which is called a tadpole, has a tail to help it swim during the early part of its life. As the tadpole gets older and changes into an adult frog, it grows legs and the tail disappears. That is true for all

An adult tailed frog

This tadpole has both legs and a tail because it is changing into a frog.

frogs. So what about the tailed frog? Male tailed frogs have a small stub sticking out between their back legs. This is not a real tail, but is used when the male mates with a female frog.

Do you know...?

The tailed frog is not the only kind of frog with a structure that looks like a small tail. Four kinds of frogs that live in New Zealand have a similar structure. One of these, called Hochstetter's frog, is pictured at right.

Why does a narrow-mouthed toad live with a tarantula?

The Great Plains narrow-mouthed toad

Narrow-mouthed toads share their nest with tarantulas.

Great Plains narrow-mouthed toads live in dry areas of North America. The toads rest in mud cracks, under stones, or in the nests of spiders called tarantulas. The spiders are big enough to kill the toads, but they leave their guests alone. The spiders even protect the toads from snakes and other predators. Why? The toads protect the spiders' babies by eating any ants that may invade the nest.

How do gastric-brooding frogs give birth?

Gastric-brooding frogs live in Australian streams. The word gastric means "stomach." As strange as it may seem, gastric-brooding frogs grow their babies in their stomachs—and then give birth to them through their mouths! The mom swallows her eggs as soon as she lays them. She does not eat until the tadpoles hatch. Once the tadpoles have grown into tiny froglets, they crawl up their mom's throat and hop out of her mouth.

A paperclip shows how small an adult gastric-brooding frog is. This frog and paperclip are shown larger than actual size!

Do you know...?

Darwin frogs (left) do not swallow their eggs, but once the tadpoles hatch, their dad picks them up in his mouth. The tadpoles change into froglets inside their dad's mouth—and then hop away!

How does the Australian water-holding frog survive drought?

Without some water nearby, most frogs dry out and die. However, Australian water-holding frogs can survive for months without water. They live in shallow pools that fill with water when it is

An Australian water-holding frog

raining but dry out at other times. When the rains stop, the frogs dig into the ground with the bony spades on their hind feet. Once in their den, the outer layer of the skin comes loose to make a bag full of sticky slime. This covering, or cocoon, keeps the frogs damp in the dry ground, where they stay through the dry season. When heavy rain falls again, it softens the ground, and the frogs climb back to the surface. There they lay their eggs in shallow water. The tadpoles grow fast and leave the water before it dries up.

Do you know...?

Australia's Aboriginal people know how to get a drink even in the driest places—they dig up water-holding frogs. The people stamp on the ground to fool the frog into thinking the rains have started. That makes the frog croak. Once dug up, a gentle squeeze will break the frog's cocoon and release some cool water.

Which frog gets smaller as it grows up?

The paradoxical frog lives in marshes in South America. When scientists first discovered this frog, they found that the adult frogs were shorter than the tadpoles. How can that be true? Most kinds of frogs change from tadpoles into tiny froglets that still have some growing to do. But paradoxical frog tadpoles grow very long—to more than 8 inches (20 cm). Most of this is the tail. The tadpole's body—less than 3 inches (8 cm) long—is the full size for an adult. When the frogs change into adults, they lose their long tail, leaving the rest of the body about the same size.

An adult paradoxical frog

Do you know...?

Paradoxical frogs are fierce hunters. In parts of Brazil, the frogs attack rain frogs. These little frogs live in large groups in water. The paradoxical frogs watch their prey from the bank, waiting for the right time to dive in for the kill.

Why is the marsupial frog like a kangaroo?

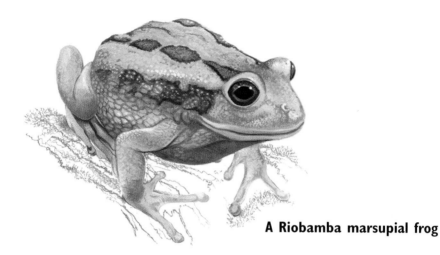

A Riobamba marsupial frog

A marsupial is a kind of mammal. Kangaroos and koalas are marsupials. Female marsupials carry their young in a pouch on their belly. Riobamba marsupial frog moms do something similar—they carry their eggs and tadpoles in a pouch on their back. The pouch's opening faces the frog's hind end. The female lays her eggs, and the male pokes them into her pouch with his feet. The eggs hatch into tadpoles in the pouch.

Do you know...?

Like many other species, male marsupial frogs attract mates with loud calls. But the clucking call of the Riobamba marsupial frog sounds more like a chicken than a frog!

How do tree frogs climb so well?

A map tree frog

There are more than 800 kinds of tree frogs in the world. Many of them spend their whole life in trees and never climb down to the ground. Tree frogs have long legs and long fingers and toes with suckers at the ends. These suckers allow the frogs to grip onto smooth and slippery surfaces, such as waxy leaves.

Common European tree frog

Which frogs can kill a person?

Poison dart frogs' bright patterns are a warning to other animals: "You can look, but don't touch!" The skin of a poison dart frog contains very strong poisons. These will kill anything that eats, or even licks, the frog. South American Indians use the skins of the frogs to make poisons to coat their hunting arrows. That is how the frogs got their name.

A blue poison dart frog's bright colors are a warning to other animals.

Do you know...?

The orange poison dart frog lives in Colombia. It is the most poisonous frog of all. Its skin is 20 times more poisonous than the skin of any other poison dart frog.

A strawberry poison dart frog

What is the edible frog?

Like sheep, cattle, and pigs, edible frogs have been bred by people. They are a cross between a pool frog and a marsh frog. Edible frogs are raised in farms and their meat is

A male edible frog croaks with two throat sacs.

throat sac

supplied to restaurants. Edible frogs spend most of their time in or near the water. They often bask in sunshine, but they jump into the water if they are disturbed.

An edible frog in a pond

Do you know...?

Have you ever eaten a frog? The meat tastes a bit like chicken and a little like fish. People cook just the frog's legs (right)—the rest of the body is not very meaty. Edible frogs' legs are often eaten in France. Other kinds of frogs are cooked in other parts of the world.

How do giant African bullfrogs protect their young?

When the rains arrive, it is time for giant African bullfrogs to mate. Females choose to mate with the largest males, and the moms lay eggs in a small pool. It is the male's job to

A giant African bullfrog eats a rat.

Do you know...?

Bushveld rain frogs only have a short time to mate each year. The males make sure they get their mates by coating their bellies in glue and sticking themselves to the females.

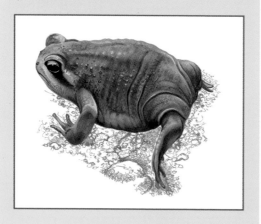

guard the eggs and the tadpoles once they hatch. Big males mate with several females, and their pools are filled with young. The tadpoles are cannibals—they eat each other! If the pool begins to dry out, the males will dig an escape channel to the nearest source of water.

Where do shovel-nosed frog tadpoles grow up?

A shovel-nosed frog

Shovel-nosed frogs spend most of their lives underground. They only come aboveground to find a mate and lay eggs. The male and female dig a

Do you know...?

Bush squeakers live in the bushveld of South Africa (below). Their habitat is very dry for much of the year and there is no water for tadpoles to swim in, so bush squeakers do not have a tadpole stage. Instead, the eggs grow directly into tiny froglets. Some bush squeakers might live their whole lives without ever swimming in water!

burrow for the eggs next to a pool. The female stays with the eggs and the tadpoles once they hatch. She coats them with foam to stop them from drying out. When it starts to rain, it is time to move. The mother frog digs a slide for the tadpoles to slip into the nearby pool.

Are glass frogs actually see-through?

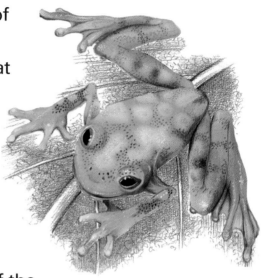

Glass frogs live in the trees of Central American forests. A glass frog's skin is so thin that you can see the animal's internal organs through it. That is where the frog gets its name. The fingers and toes are completely see-through and have the same color as whatever the frog is standing on. The main part of the body is green, which camouflages the frog on leaves.

A Valerio's glass frog rests on a leaf.

Do you know...?

Casque-headed frogs also live in the mountain forests of Central and South America. They are named for the armor plates and points on their head and back. These features help the little frogs hide among leaves. Some casque-headed frogs live in trees, while others live among the fallen leaves on the forest floor.

Do lungless salamanders ever get out of breath?

Salamanders are amphibians. When in water, young salamanders breathe using gills, like a fish. On land, most salamanders take breaths of air into their lungs.

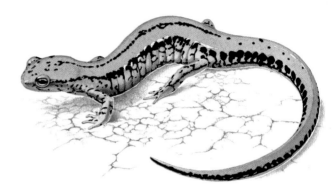

A lungless three-lined salamander

Some salamanders don't have gills or lungs. These salamanders live in and close to streams packed with oxygen—a vital gas that fuels the body. The oxygen passes through the skin and into the salamanders' blood. This system works out of the water as well, as long as the skin is kept moist.

Do you know...?

A hellbender is a salamander that lives in the eastern United States. Scientists have found that a hellbender does not die if its lungs are removed. It gets enough oxygen through its skin from the clear stream water in which it lives.

Do axolotls ever grow up?

The axolotl (*ah-hoh-loh-tol*) is a kind of salamander that lives in Mexico. Young salamanders begin life in water, where they breathe through feathery gills. Young salamanders are called larvae.

gills

An adult axolotl

Axolotl larvae are similar to the young of other salamanders. However, larvae usually lose their gills and live on land when they are grown. Axolotls do not do this—the adults look more or less the same as the larvae. The only difference is that the adults have reproductive organs, so they can breed.

Do you know...?

The axolotl is not the only type of salamander to never grow into a land-living adult. Several other species will also put off turning into an adult if the water they live in is too cold. Mole salamanders (above) might take

years to make the change. In northern areas, where it never gets warm enough, these salamanders stay in water for their whole lives.

A two-toed Congo eel, or amphiuma

Are Congo eels really eels from the Congo?

The Congo is a forested region of Central Africa. A huge river system also called the Congo flows through the forest. Eels are fish that have long, snakelike bodies, so it may come as a surprise to learn that Congo eels are not eels, and they don't live in the Congo River. They are long, thin salamanders that live in swamps in the southern United States. There, they prey on crayfish, frogs, snails, and even snakes.

Do you know...?

Caecilians are amphibians that look more like worms than salamanders or frogs. Caecilians do not have legs, and most are burrowing hunters that prey on worms. Some swim in swamps and eat small fish. These water-dwelling caecilians (right) are called rubber eels.

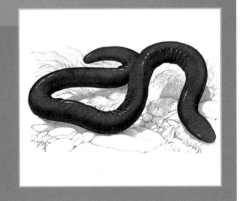

Do olms ever see daylight?

Olms are salamanders that live only in flooded caves in a region of Europe called the Dalmatian coast. In the deep caves,

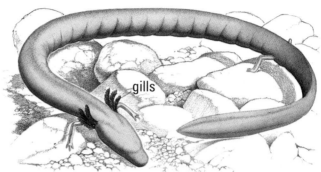

An olm breathes through gills behind the head.

there is no daylight, and an olm has no need for sight. Therefore, the animal's eyes are buried deep in the skin on its head. In the total darkness, there is also no need for the olm to have a pattern on its skin. Instead, the olm's skin has no coloring in it, and the blood running inside makes the olm look pale pink. If an olm is taken out of a cave and exposed to sunlight, it gradually changes to black over several weeks.

Do you know...?

Waterdogs, or mudpuppies, are tough salamanders that cannot survive out of water. They live in eastern North America and remain active hunters in cold weather, even if their pool freezes over. Waterdogs are thought to produce a squeaky bark, although they are usually quiet animals.

Why is a slimy salamander so slimy?

A slimy salamander

Slimy salamanders are covered in a thick, glutinous (sticky) slime. This slime is produced by glands at the base of the tail. Most salamanders have these glands. They squirt a foul-tasting liquid when the animal is under attack. Slimy salamanders produce more liquid than most, and the liquid is very sticky. If the liquid gets into a predator's mouth or eyes, it is very hard to remove.

Do you know...?

Slimy salamanders and their relatives perform an elaborate dance before they mate. The male presses his chin against the female's body. He then rests on his tail and lifts his hind legs up and down. The female then follows him around until he drops a packet of his reproductive cells. The female uses his reproductive cells to fertilize her eggs.

Are fire salamanders dangerous?

The fire salamander's flame-yellow color may have reminded the ancient Romans of fire. However, the color was actually a warning of another type of danger—behind the fire salamander's eyes are large poison glands. When the salamander is attacked, holes, or pores, in the glands open wide and a sticky, milklike liquid flows out. The same poison comes out of smaller glands on the back. The salamander uses these smaller glands to squirt poison at prey by arching its back.

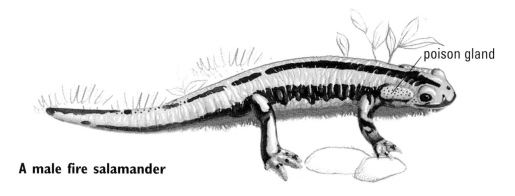

poison gland

A male fire salamander

Do you know...?

Japanese fire-bellied newts are brightly colored salamanders. Their colors warn enemies of their nasty, poisonous skin. However, the warning sign is only really visible from below, making it most obvious to fish that hunt them.

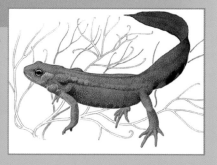

Glossary

anuran: a frog or toad

camouflage: a coloration or body shape that helps an animal blend with—and hide in—its surroundings

cannibal: an animal that eats others of its own kind

fertilize: when the female and male sex cells join up. Fertilization is necessary for new amphibian life to be created.

froglet: a young frog that has changed from a tadpole and grown legs, but which has not yet become an adult

gill: a breathing organ used by many kinds of animals that live in water to get oxygen. Young amphibians have gills.

gland: a part of the body that produces a substance for a specific use

habitat: a particular kind of environment, such as a forest or a lake

marsupial: mammals in which the females carry their young in a pouch

organ: a group of body tissues working together to perform vital functions. The heart is an organ.

oxygen: a gas that animals must breathe to survive

predator: an animal that hunts other animals for food

prey: an animal that is hunted by another animal

snout: an animal's nose and jaws

species: a group of animals that share features, and can mate and produce young together

Find Out More

Books about amphibians

Clark, Barry. *Amphibian*. New York: DK Children, 2005.

Gilpin, Daniel. *Tree Frogs, Mud Puppies, and Other Amphibians*. Mankato, MN: Compass Point Books, 2006.

Kalman, Bobbie, and Jacqueline Langille. *What Is an Amphibian?* New York: Crabtree Publishing, 2000.

Moffett, Mark. *Face to Face with Frogs*. Des Moines, IA: National Geographic Children's Books, 2008.

Phillips, Dee. *Reptiles and Amphibians*. Minnetonka, MN: Two-Can Publishing, 2006.

Stewart, Melissa. *Amphibians*. New York: Children's Press, 2000.

Useful websites

Amphibians
animals.nationalgeographic.com/animals/amphibians.html

Amphibians: What Are They?
kidstuff.homestead.com

Frogland
allaboutfrogs.org/froglnd.shtml

Understanding Amphibians
www.animalweb.com/an-amphibians.asp

Index